The Krown of Keter

ISBN-13: 978-1478239550

DEDICATION

To the future of Creation.

Table of Contents

THE KROWN OF KETER

Acknowledgements

Prologue

The STORY

Chapter 1-Special Day

Chapter 2-Wishing for Water

Chapter 3-Fallen Kingdom

Chapter 4-Secret Spring

Chapter 5-Finally...a Cold Drink

Chapter 6-A Quest

Chapter 7-Finding the First Clue

Chapter 8-The Second Clue

Chapter 9-The Tablet of Hermes

Chapter 10-The Gift of Daath

Chapter 11-The Power

Chapter 12-The Perfect Wish

Chapter 13-War Breaks Out

Chapter 14-The Imbalance

Chapter 15-Canceling the First Wish

Chapter 16-Tired and Hungry

Chapter 17-Harnessing the Power of the Tablet

Chapter 18-Luke Studies the Book

Chapter 19-Lucy Hears Tapping

Chapter 20-Lucy's Dream

Chapter 21-Tipareth

Chapter 22-The REAL Perfect Wish

Chapter 23-The Royal Family

Chapter 24-Empty Bellies and a Daughter's Wish

Chapter 25-The Second Wish

Chapter 26-The Krown of Keter

The End

The Beginning

About the Author

About the Artist

Other Books by author

Acknowledgements

First of all I'd like to thank Kaye Brookland for her generous editing support over the years and Anne Leslie who got the ball rolling for this tale, by showing up each week to share our writing experiences. I am truly indebted to Joan Paul for her inspiring paintings. The water spirits picture and the hovel painting were conceived years before this story but were woven in with the newer ones of the trees and the peddler and the giantess. I owe a great debt of gratitude to Rose and Gordon Burke and Oliver Flecknell for their technical support with the photos. I'm so thankful as well for the Wilmot Writers Group who have listened to and read the story and contributed comments and ideas. Bless the kids: Laughlin, Taela, Mallory and of course my granddaughter Olivia, who took the time and interest in this tale. I'd also like to thank my wife Sally for the patience she's shown when I cursed and cried in frustration over formatting.

A word about this tale.

You have actually received two stories for the price of one.

The italics are the telling in the Future and the rest is the FIRST Story.

Let's keep it going until it IS history.

Prologue

When his grandmother laid her knitting aside, Jody Jack looked up from the book he was reading. He nudged his sister with his foot. Jessie Mae was lying on her stomach on the Rainbow rag rug that covered most of the floor of the Ready Room. They had made a plan together that morning to convince their grandmother to give them the Story. Jessie looked at him with her big green eyes. She sat up after rubbing the grit off the clay coloured skin of her elbows; crossing her legs and smiled with excitement. They both slid across the rug to their elder's feet in one smooth motion. Looking up into her eyes they begged, "Grandmother Bina, will you give us the Story again?" The old woman took a deep breath and studied the picture on the far wall as she considered their request. Once more in unison (which happened often, as they were twins) the children pleaded,

"Please Grand Mother?" Jessie Mae reached out and touched her elder's arm and looked wistfully into her golden eyes and spoke, "Please tell us about the olden days. After all, it is our birthday at midnight. The tale would be the very best gift."

With a twinkle in her eyes now, she looked at Jessie and asked, "Which story do you wish to hear?"

Jodie Jack chuckled, "You know the one .The story about when the world forgot we were all One Family."

The wise woman pretended to finally recall the Story requested. Jody Jack rolled his eyes and shook his head at the antics of the white haired woman. He pulled a bright red ripe apple from the bowl on the small table beside him and after polishing it for a few seconds on his shirt, laid it on the small window ledge. His twin went across the room and dipped a small cup into a pail of water and placed it too on the sill beside the apple.

The ancient woman began by reaching for the cup of tea beside her. Then she took a mouthful of the dark fluid and moaned in pleasure on swallowing it. She pushed on the floor with her feet and started to rock in the alder rocking chair. Meeting Jody Jack's eyes, she began the Story.

The Story

Terrified and blocking his ears with his hands to muffle the roar of gunfire, Luke crouched beside a large green mossy boulder. His throat burned from the smoke of the fires raging in the brush all around him. Through straining stinging eyes, Luke thought he spied a pair of eyes, in the head shaped stone at the mouth of the stream. Squinting and wiping water from his eyes with his sleeve, the boy studied the weird stone again. Now he saw only a simple rock.

They both jumped as a large chunk of ice fell off the roof, as always they were a bit scared at the beginning of the Story because they had never lived in a world where war was happening. It was only a thing read about in the history books they sometimes found in the library.

When the forest at last became quiet, (so quiet it was as scary as the earsplitting noise earlier), the brown haired child dared rise and use his shelter as a seat. While he looked around, he was able to hear the

burbling gurgling water flowing out of the pond into the brook, but strangely, no bird song. Then Luke heard a voice. It was a soft female voice, barely audible above the sounds of the stream. He scanned the clearing for its source but found no one. He was alone. Just moments earlier, terrified deer, coyotes and rabbits had screamed howled and scattered. Luke was certain he was alone. Looking down in the streambed again, he clearly saw a pair of eyes and mouth in the rock on the edge of the water. Incredibly, the mouth moved and a small frail voice spoke, "Luke, please help us. Only you and your sister can save OUR world!"As the creature of the stone spoke, the boy was shocked to see that there were many faces in those rocks staring at him with sad pleading eyes.

Then a bullet whizzed by Luke's ear, close enough for him to feel its breeze. He dropped to the ground and wrapped himself once more around the granite boulder. Closing his eyes, the boy pressed his face into the thick mat of moss and clung until he felt something huge, land on his back. As he tensed he shouted. "Help!", and woke up to find himself safely in his own room

Chapter 1

Special Day

Lucy opened her turquoise blue eyes, rolled over and looked at the calendar. At last the sun had come up on the final Sunday of August. She jumped out of bed and scrambled around tossing her clothes over her shoulder, while brushing long black hair. Passing her brother's room she aimed a pillow at his head. From under the quilt, Luke shouted, "Help!"

"Come on Luke, stop playing around. It's time to get up!" she coaxed as she continued down to the privy to dress.

Most days, Luke dreaded morning, but he was happy when he opened his brown eyes today for two reasons; first, the relief to be safe from the nightmare, and second, because he remembered that this was going to be the day of the annual Hamamelis harvest. Because Abba had explained so clearly the Latin name for Witch Hazel Luke remembered that it meant, "together" + "fruit" because the flowers and fruits are on the plant at the same time. Each summer, the children looked forward to this event. Ama always packed a yummy picnic lunch for the foragers and it was a special time and adventure with their abba.

The tradition began when Luke was four years old and Lucy five. They would leave home at daylight. As they walked along a familiar path, Abba reminded them the names of many of the plants they saw. He also explained the ways of preserving some of these plants for food or medicine. Early on they learned to be ever so quiet while walking in the woods, and were often rewarded with glimpses of birds and animals that noisy children would never get a peek at.

This year was even more exciting because, for the very first time, they were given permission to take this trip on their own. Abba was too sick with the flu to come with them, so, as they were now aged ten and eleven, Ama decided that they were old enough to go without a grown-up.

It was now mid-morning and they stopped in the usual meadow to have the rest and drink as was their habit. When Lucy pulled the draw string open and dug through the contents of the maroon coloured lunch bag, her eyes got wide and her mouth flew open with a gasp as she demanded, "Where's the water bottle? Ama told you to fill it and pack it Luke!"

Luke shook his wildly curly head and replied, "No, Ama told You, to pack it."

"Well, it doesn't matter who was supposed to or not. We can't go all day without water. We'll be too thirsty to work.

Chapter 2

Wishing for Water

So they took their mid-morning break, sitting quietly with gloomy thoughts of giving up this special day, over a foolish mistake. Luke wished he had a magic wand, which he could wave and make a jug of water appear. Lucy was parched. She began trying to think of ways they could get around this problem of no water without returning home. We need to find a spring, she thought. In her memory she went over the path, trying to recall if there were any cottages along the way that might have a well. Her mouth felt like she had been eating unbuttered popcorn. She remembered there were no wells, as no people lived along the stream the witch hazel gathering path followed.

Luke's freckled face suddenly brightened. "I know what we can do," he said. "We can cut a twitching stick."

Lucy looked at him with confusion and asked, "A what?" "

A twitching stick," he answered. "It's a hazel wood branch used to find water." And then she remembered what Abba had shown them last year on their journey here.

"Right. Great idea Luke! "

So off they went to find the place where the path from the road connected with the stream. They knew that was where they would find the best branch, as hazel grows beside streams. This was also the starting point of the hazelnut harvest each year. Lucy watched as Luke selected a Y shaped branch, and held it with his arms outstretched. Both hands were wrapped around the single end, and the forked ends were pointing away from him. She pictured Abba holding the bough reversed with the point of the switch outward and the two forked ends gripped palms up. She asked, "Are you sure the branch was pointing that way? I thought the single end was pointed out." She said it kindly, knowing if she was bossy, he could be quite stubborn.

Luke closed his eyes and tried to picture how Abba had held the stick last year. Nodding, he opened his eyes and looked up at Lucy smiling, "You're right, I am holding it backwards. What a goof!" He laughed at himself. Then he grasped the stick by the forked ends, his palms up and elbows against his body.

The bushes were just beginning to turn the yellow, orange red and rusty brown shades of fall. It wasn't long before the tip of the hazel branch began to point down. The closer Luke walked to the brook the more the switch in his hand trembled against his palms and pulled toward the ground. He looked up at Lucy and grinned, "Of course. The stream is water, but how will we find a fresh spring?"They both knew that water rising up from underground was usually safe to drink but they might get very sick if they drank water that was lying still on top of the ground.

At this point Grand Mother Bina stopped. She looked at Jody Jack and asked, "Was it always safe to drink water flowing up from underground?" Jody Jack considered this for a few moments scratching his chin.

Then he answered, "No!"

Grand Mother nodded looking at Jessie Mae and asked, "Why"?

Shaking her head, the girl chimed in, "Because they forgot that water was Mother Earth's Blood and put poison into it."

"Who put poison in it?"Grand Mother Bina asked.

"The Profiters", replied Jessie Mae.

The wrinkled woman turned to Jody Jack again and said, "So what? There was lots of water." Again the kids knew the woman was acting out with them.

The twins jumped in at once, "But we are One with the Earth because we are Made of Her. Whatever is in Her blood is in our blood".

"Oh", answered the woman pretending to 'get it', once more. Then she started up again...

They stopped and let out a frustrated sigh in unison. Lucy said "Well it's my turn to use the switch, let's see if I can do any better." He passed his sister the stick. She took a deep breath and heaved out a huge sigh as she gripped the twitching stick. She deliberately turned her back on the stream to avoid the earlier problem. After what seemed like an hour, she thought about giving up but then she had the idea to go into the forest and off the beaten path. Luke shook his head silently and hoped that his sister wouldn't get them lost in the woods.

Hearing a branch snap in the bushes behind them, they froze. Lucy looked into Luke's eyes and they waited. Luke wondered if they were about to get a look at the wild creature caught stalking them. He imagined a deer or a rabbit watching from the shadows, blending in with the shade of the bushes around them, waiting silently for him and his sister to move on so it could continue with its travels.

Then they heard, 'Meow. Meow? They turned and looked behind them to discover that Kajiji, their pet cat had been following them. They giggled and Luke ran over and petted the calico animal saying, "So you figured you'd come along and keep an eye on us huh? Silly kitty." He kneeled down and scratched the cat behind the ears while Kajiji purred happily and leaned into his rubbing.

Chapter 3

Fallen Kingdom

Shortly after they entered into the shadow of the forest, their path was blocked by a huge fallen tree. The tree might have been considered a 'deadfall' by some, but Abba called it a 'nurse tree', because it was a nursery for many life forms as its bark rotted. One fifth of the forest creatures depend on these trees for food and homes. There were at least three types of moss and lichen and between the ground and the air around them, were insects of all shapes and sizes, from beetles to dragon flies. Toadstools and other fungi decorated not only the fallen tree but also the nearby forest floor with a variety of yellows, oranges, reds and purples.

As Luke spied this array of colours he remembered Ama telling him that fungi were neither plant nor animal but something in between. They are closer to animals than plants and classified as eukarya. Ama had said, "Imagine if the fungi could translate the wisdom of the trees into animal, (which is what we are)." Ama had also said that pine trees can live a thousand years. WOW! A thousand years. Luke sighed in awe. This was an ancient pine tree, for sure. He looked it over and wondered if it could be that old.

Luke and Lucy began their journey over the fallen tree. Because it was so long, a trip to where the top or smallest part of the tree lay would take longer than going over base of the trunk. This crossing was difficult because it was steep to climb this mini mountain. The tree's girth (around its trunk), was over twenty feet. They had to pick their way slowly and carefully because they needed to find pathways through the branches, and look for limbs that were strong enough for them to pull themselves up with. They discovered they must step carefully as there were places where loose or missing bark made the going slippery. In other places the tree dissolved under their feet and the branches either snapped back and scratched them or slapped their faces.

Finally they got down off the other side of the tree."What a relief!" gasped Lucy. Thankfully they had made it without too many splinters or scratches. Lucy stood still with her back to the tree for a minute and then put the twitching switch into position. She began walking and then hesitated, then stepped to the left. Luke shook his head, still afraid of getting lost but followed her lead anyway.

They kept this northwest direction for several minutes until they heard Kajiji Meowing. Knowing this may mean, "Look Out", they stopped. The twitching stick turned sharply down towards the ground. They scanned the area all around them. They saw a maze of trees and bushes and then heard the sound of moving water. They knew the stream was too far away from them to hear. "Well", Lucy said, "We know there is water underground here somewhere. Since we can hear it, it must come up and out close by."

Luke turned to Kajiji and said, "Thanks for helping us find water kitty. What would we do without you?"This wasn't the first time Kajiji showed them her wisdom. She often told them the best spot to drop their fishing line in, or where to find the ripest berries and one time even helped them get home when they were lost in the woods. But they never asked her for assistance, because she was a cat, and she only did what she wanted to do because she wanted to do it.

Chapter 4

Secret Spring

They came upon a giant weeping willow tree. Because willow trees love to have their roots in water, Luke knew this was another sign there must be lots of water nearby. They made their way through the thousands of yellow branches that filled the space for forty feet around. This was an old grandmother willow. The children knew much comfort had come from Her bark because it was used to make a medicine like Aspirin that takes away pain. The scars on the tree's bark were reminders of what She had given to humans. Doing what Lucy had been taught by her grand abba, she took a small embroidered cloth bag out her pocket. Pulling the drawstring open she reached in and pulled out a pinch of cornmeal. She sprinkled this at the willow's roots. As she made this offering of precious food, Lucy thanked the old willow for all She had given.

Luke noticed that a few feet away there was a large mound of something. He started off to examine it. As he got closer he saw the top sixteen inches of a large wooden barrel coming up from the ground. They noticed a pathway of flagstones set into the wet hunter green moss which they followed up to the barrel. Peering within they saw a fresh spring bubbling up. A hole in the side of the barrel let the overflow run out into a mossy bog around the spring.

Lucy stood beside her brother, her face full of joy. She wondered how this spring could be here in the middle of the forest, all by itself. There seemed to be no remains of earlier settlement here. They saw no old dug out basements or leftover root cellars usually found around areas where people had once lived. Who would have gone to all the work of digging this spring out and putting the barrel here? She looked over at Luke who was looking at it with the same questioning eyes.

Chapter 5

Finally … a Cold Drink

The energy burned by the morning travels suddenly caught up with them and put both of their tummies on the empty button. Lucy said, "I'm starved! Let's eat."

Luke said, "Let's have a drink first. I'm so dry I think I might blow away."

He chuckled and smiled as she said, "I don't think that's too likely Lukey." That's the name she called him when he was a toddler.

She was one year older than he, but she seemed at least several years older much of the time. He was an "action" person and she was a, "let's think about this for a bit," kind of person. So he often went off half-cocked and she was often paralyzed by more thinking than doing until the doing time was past. She missed out on many of his great adventures because of this. He on the other hand, often paid a high price for jumping into situations that were beyond his power and getting into trouble. For instance, the time he got into the hornets' nest while climbing up into the shed roof. It never occurred to him that once he was on the roof the hornets could have at him freely. Thank goodness Lucy happened to hear him and came with the ladder to save him. He was in too much pain to be embarrassed, so he thanked her over and over again. But Lucy missed out on fun the night he and his friend Mike had gone down to the field by the pond and watched the meteor shower. It was the most brilliant light show he'd ever seen. He saw the regret on her face when he talked about it over breakfast the next day.

Deciding she was also very thirsty, Lucy joined Kajiji and Luke beside the spring. The cat was lapping up water from the overflow area on the ground. A copper dipper was hung on a small hook fastened to the wooden barrel. As their thirst had built since breakfast, the water was cold and deliciously sweet. Lucy pointed at the bright mosaic of colours made by the noon day sun's reflection on the water's surface. There were bits of; white, blue, yellows and greens mirrored from the sky and tree above. As the spring bubbled up from the ground, it shattered the surface, and the fragments of colour disappeared as they floated up over the edge of the barrel. Luke nodded politely but was far more interested in getting into his lunch than seeing the show.

Lucy had spotted another large fallen tree. This one was covered with thick shamrock green moss. After satisfying her thirst, she went to the log and set out lunch. They gobbled the bread and apples Ama had wrapped up for them this morning. While they ate, Kajiji entertained them cavorting about, chasing after butterflies and pouncing on leaves that fell from the branches above. After clapping for the cat's show, each child pinched off a piece of their cheese for her. She was not too interested at first, but after sniffing it, she ate it up and licked her lips looking for more. The children would save their best treat, the biscuits and marble berry jelly for their late afternoon snack. They always stopped on the way home at the place where the stream connected to the path to the lane and had a short rest and a nibble to get them through until supper. They both took another long drink and Luke was on his way back to the giant tree trunk when he heard Lucy call his name.

Chapter 6

A Quest

He turned and saw she was pointing to a board attached to the side of the barrel. When Lucy stopped to have a last drink she noticed a wooden plaque on the outside of the barrel. She read the plaque to Luke.

"If you can fetch the Krown of Keter two wishes you will be granted.

Three triangles you need to find and the answer will be planted.

For the first wish be my guest, get the second at the end of the quest."

Luke's face lit up with glee. "Cool!" He said excitedly "A quest! Just like in the stories Ama tells us." Of course Luke wanted to charge into getting their wishes granted. It was all she could do to talk him out of rushing off and doing the wishing thing. But Lucy managed to convince him to finish the harvest first. She did this by reminding him what Abba and Ama would say if they didn't finish this job the very first time they were trusted to do it without a grown up.

With Kajiji silently at their heels, they retraced their steps to the path along the stream and began to fill the two pillowcases with the leaves and branch tips that Abba used to make medicine. They picked the lighter green tips of the hazel bushes to be made into healing ointments and salves. The leaves they gathered would be hung in a dark dry place until they dried. Then they would be stored in glass containers until needed to make medicine. While they sweated and strained and swatted at bugs, their thoughts see-sawed back and forth between the pride of gathering the leaves that would soothe aches and pains and possible wishes they would make, if they succeeded on the Quest. Luke carefully snapped hand width sized twigs off the tips of branches while Lucy carefully tucked them into the two pillowcases. This was a routine they had settled into over the years. They took only a few branches from each tree so that it would survive to produce more next year. They finished the harvest and decided to go straight home rather than stop for a snack and a rest. They were in a hurry to get back, almost bursting with the story about their amazing discovery.

When they got within sight of the house they started shouting for Ama to come out and meet them. They could hardly contain themselves and each one took a turn excitedly filling in the details of their adventure of finding fresh water in the middle of the woods and the best part, which was the promise of thrills if they succeeded in the Quest. Luke squealed, "Two wishes granted! Wow! Isn't it exiting Ama?"

At the supper table that evening they discovered that Abba was almost over his bout with the flu. Luke gobbled down beans and cornbread as he tried to get a word in edgewise whenever Lucy stopped to take bite or a breath. Abba and Ama looked at each other secretly across the large wooden table.

Lucy declared, "Isn't it exciting! Abba, Ama? Can you think of anything or a place with a three triangle symbol on it? Ama scratched her head and rubbed her tired eyes and looked up to the ceiling as she tried to remember. Luke said, "Abba, do you know of anything with that symbol?"

Abba replied, "Yes, I believe I do. But right now I'm really tired and I can't think of it. Give me a good night's rest, and maybe I can remember what it is or where it is, OK?" Luke and Lucy looked at their Abba hopefully and nodded in unison.

They helped Abba clear up the dishes and then they washed up for bed. The children discussed their day and tried to come up with a plan for the morning. Climbing into the small loft, they giggled as they chatted about how bad things could have gone today, if they had gotten lost in the woods instead of finding the spring.

Chapter 7

Finding the First Clue

At breakfast they were excited to hear if Abba or Ama had remembered anything about the three triangle sign. Ama still couldn't remember, but promised to keep trying. After finishing his morning writing and meditation, Abba finally looked up from his book to the children with a grave expression. "Your quest could be dangerous and I want you to promise me that if something happens that you think you can't handle, you'll come to Ama and me for help. OK?"

Lucy and Luke looked at each other with fear and then back to Abba and responded together, "Yes Abba."

Abba let out a long heavy sigh and went on, "Look on the top shelf of the book case in the back room. That symbol may be on a cover." The children bolted from the room. They couldn't reach the top shelf, so Lucy and her brother worked together to drag the heavy wooden chair from the next room in beside the bookshelf. In their rush to climb up and be the first to reach the books, they almost knocked each other down. Luckily, they discovered that if they helped the other balance, they could both fit on the back of the chair.

The books were covered in a thick layer of dust. Cobwebs decorated the corners of the room that they wouldn't have noticed, had they not been so high. They looked at each title on the shelf. Luke said, "Abba said it's on the cover. I wonder if we'll have to take each one out to find the sign." Lucy scanned the row in front of them. Finally she spotted a spine with no words on it, only some kind of picture. She picked it up so that she could get a closer look. The spine had a picture of a crown and the triple triangle symbol. Just as she shouted, "This is it Luke!" she was almost knocked off the chair by Luke's humungous sneeze. The book fell from her hand onto the floor. She scrambled down off the chair, declaring between her giggles, "We found it! We found it!" Luke jumped off the arm of the old chair and dove at the book trying to wrench it from his sister's hands. Lucy was having no part of this. She had seen it first, so she felt she should get the first look.

When she finally did pull open its pages she was disappointed and so was Luke. The book was mostly all in symbols. There was only a readable word here and there. There were squiggly lines and weird shapes and tangled lines. On the first page there was a picture of an old fashioned oil lamp with the letters BINA on it, and the triple triangle sign on its base. On the following page was a green rectangle, with two arrows within its face. One arrow pointed up, the other down. In the centre of this rectangle were the words, 'As Above, So Below'. On the top of the page was written 'The Tablet of Hermes'.

The children spent the rest of the morning poring over the pages of the book. At lunch they showed their morning's find to Abba. He seemed as puzzled as they were by the symbols on the pages. Lucy asked, "Where did this book come from Abba?"

Abba answered, "I'm not sure. I remember seeing it when we first moved into this house."

Luke looked at Ama and inquired, "Any luck Ama?"

She shook her head sadly. "Let me see this book." She reached out and took the book examining the cover. When she saw the triangle symbol she stopped and studied it. Then she opened the book. When she saw a picture of a lamp she exclaimed, "Yes. I know now! That lamp. That lamp is in the cellar. It was there when we moved in." They didn't even wait for directions. Luke flung open the trap door in the kitchen floor then he and Lucy jumped down the ladder rungs into the cellar. They both sprung off the fourth rung from the bottom onto the dirt floor.

Abba grumbled, 'It's a wonder one of them doesn't slip and break a bone, the way they race down that ladder.".

After she heard them land safely at the bottom, Ama exhaled a tense breath and walked over to the cellar door and said, "It's on the shelf outside the cold room."

The children stopped in front of the shelf where they saw the dusty lamp. Luke bumped several spider webs pulling it down. They returned to the kitchen, and Ama passed Luke a cleaning rag to wipe the dust from the base of the lamp, and gave Lucy one to clean the shade of the lamp. Luke polished down to the triangle symbol on the lamp.

Abba coughed at all the dust and said, "Well that's enough adventure for today. It's time you young people got to your chores. Luke, you know what you need to do. Get those cucumbers picked, cut up and ready for pickles. Lucy, it's your turn to muck out the chicken house."

The kids frowned, moaned and protested, but got into their work clothes and did as they were told.

Chapter 8

The Second Clue

By supper time the work was finished and the children came in famished. They washed their hands and dove into their supper. After clearing up the dishes, the children once again took up the book, staring and squinting over its pages, trying to understand the meaning of the mysterious symbols. After several hours, the candles flickered and Ama announced it was time for bed. Both children tossed and turned that night with excitement about the next day's adventures.

In the morning over a breakfast of pancakes and apple juice, Abba and Ama smiled slyly at each other, while the children tried to puzzle out what the strange glyphs in the book might mean. Finally Ama spoke, "Children", upon getting their complete attention she smiled and began. "After you went to bed last night, when the candles got so low we could hardly see to read, we decided to fill that old lamp that you brought upstairs yesterday morning. Well, when we looked at that book under the light of the lamp, the meaning of the symbols became clear."

Chapter 9

The Tablet of Hermes

After gobbling down breakfast with barely any chewing, Lucy ran and grabbed the book. Abba lit the lamp and Luke rubbed his hands with delight. The children's faces shone bright from lamp and excitement as they opened the book and were able to understand its messages. They learned that to find the Krown of Keter, they must first discover the Tablet of Hermes. On the next page was a map to the tablet. There was a large X on the page, and beside it was a picture of the circle with smaller odd shapes in a line beside it.

Luke wanted to dash out the door to the adventure, but Abba stopped him and wisely suggested," Maybe you could take the book and the lamp with you; in case you need them later."Luke blushed, as he plucked the book from Abba's hand and slipped it into the backpack that was holding the lunch Ama had already prepared for them.

Ama smiled and said "Good Luck".

Lucy turned down the flame on the lamp until it disappeared. She picked it up carefully, holding it away from her body, while it cooled. Meanwhile she slipped a box of matches into her pocket. They started out down the lane to the main road. As usual, the children were quiet and observant of every tree, bird or insect they saw along their path. Luke spotted a large shiny black crow. The crow didn't fly off as they approached but instead cawed at them, as if to give them a message. They stopped for a minute and listened but as they didn't understand crow language, they continued on their way.

Not long after, they stopped while Lucy cautiously tucked the lamp into her pack and Luke pulled the book out of the bag he was carrying and opened it to the map. He pierced the page with hawk-eyed intensity, trying to remember what the lamp had revealed earlier. When he recognized that this was the path back to the spring his eyes widened and he nodded. He informed his sister of this news with glee. Excitedly he said, "Now at least we know exactly where to go". She nodded with relief. Secretly pleased and smiling, she knew from the start where the map led to, but being a generous person, because she had lead the way to the discovery of the spring, she wanted her brother to at least think, he was leading the way this time.

At last they arrived at the place on the path where Lucy had turned away from the stream and ventured into the woods two days earlier. They traveled along the straight line until seeing the giant nurse tree and followed the same route up and over it. Today, Luke noticed a patch of Indian Pipes or Ghost plant. The first time he saw this bone white plant, he thought it was a fungi, but Abba explained that this was actually a plant that had no chlorophyll. It didn't use the sun to grow, but instead was fed from its roots by surrounding plants.

When they came down the other side of the massive trunk, they scanned the forest for the old willow that marked the spring. At first they couldn't see it. But soon, Lucy spotted the pale green and yellow willow branches in the dimness of the forest. They ran to the base of the tree, and raced to see who could find the first clue to the place where the Tablet of Hermes was hiding.

They hunted high and low around the spring. They searched around the base of it. Luke picked up a fallen branch from an evergreen, and used it to sweep the dead leaves aside. This was the kind of tree that had short needles on it. Rather than changing colour and falling off in the fall it stayed green year round. They hunted desperately, making a circle of search, spiral wider and wider, until finally Luke said, "I'm starving. Let's eat lunch, then try again." Lucy wasn't happy about this idea, because it was only mid-morning, but instead of arguing, she went along with it.

She set their lunch out again on the same mossy tree trunk they used for a table the first time. They ate in silence. Luke gobbled his sandwich, but Lucy only nibbled hers with no appetite, while she continued to look around for the tablet. When the food was gone Luke went to the spring to get a drink.

Lucy went about returning her lunch container to the bag. While picking up the sandwich box, she accidently tore off a piece of the dark green moss from a section of the fallen tree. She picked it up with the intent to leave it the way it was before they were there, like her abba had taught her. But, in a moment of impulse; she peeled it back off the surface even more. She looked closely beneath where the moss had grown and saw markings that looked like they had been carved into the wood. She peeled the moss back even farther. There, engraved into the trunk of this old tree, were the symbols they were searching for, the triple triangle and one arrow pointing up, the other pointing down and, beneath it the words they had been looking for. This was the Tablet of Hermes.

Chapter 10

The Gift of Daath

"Luke", Lucy squealed. He was beside her in what seemed like a flash. Together they read the words aloud, "As above, so below."

After Luke explored the so-called tablet, he whined, "How can we take this home?"

Lucy thought for a second and then answered, "We can't. But why do we need to? We know what the words are. We can remember them."

He was not completely satisfied by her answer, but with a long sigh said, "I guess. I hope you're right."

Lucy said, "Let's see what the book says we should do now." Luke pulled the book from his sack and opened it to the page where they found the map earlier that morning. Then they remembered that the lamp must be lit in order to understand the writing. Lucy pulled it from her bag and set it on the makeshift table and pulled the pack of wooden matches from her pocket. She opened the box of matches; removed the shade from the lamp, and adjusted the wick so that she could light it. After turning the wick up, she plucked a match from the box and scratched it on a nearby rock. She carefully touched the flame to the wick and then blew out the match. As flame rose from the lamp, she turned the key to draw the wick shorter and replaced the glass shade. Luke placed the open book beside the lamp. On the page following the map, they read aloud,

"To receive the Gift of Daath,

find the tablet, light the lamp.

Three times that hour,

Repeat the words of power,

'as above, so below',

After making the first wish,

the flame must survive,

Because, when the light goes out,

so does the wishing well dry."

The children looked at each other with a mixture of fear and excitement. Lucy whispered, "Gift? What kind of gift?" Luke shook his head in shock and answered, "Who knows? We'll have to wait and see."

Chapter 11

The Power

They agreed they would share the gift, and repeat the magic words on the count of three. They solemnly repeated the phrase, "As above, so below" three times. Suddenly the wind appeared out of nowhere and whipped the branches of the willow around their heads.

Then a large animal charged through the trees not far from them. They heard a flock of birds noisily launching from a nearby maple tree. It began raining and then hailing. There was the strong smell of sulfur in the air. Lucy checked to make sure the lamp had not blown out. Luke remembered his dream from that morning as he shouted above the racket around them, "As above so below, stop!" Everything was suddenly still.

Lucy looked at Luke and hugged him. "Wow! Luke that was great", she said. "How did you know?"

He sheepishly replied, "I didn't. I just took a wild guess that if speaking the words could cause all that commotion, then maybe the same words would make it stop it".

The hubbub reminded him of his bad dream, so Luke suggested, "I think I've had all the adventure I can handle in one day. Maybe we should go home and ask Ama and Abba to help us figure out the best wish. Its gonna be dark soon." Lucy nodded in agreement as she picked up the lamp and turned the wick down until the flame went out. Luke replaced the book into his backpack and they started home. Lucy put forth, "I think that we should spend the night thinking about what we will wish for." Luke responded "Great idea Luc!"

Then they heard a thunderous Boom, Boom, and Boom from a distance growing louder every second. They felt the ground quake and shake beneath them. At first, when they looked around the forest they could see nothing unusual except for the leaves trembling on the branches as the presence approached. Then they heard trees snapping and sensed something huge getting closer and closer to them. Finally they saw what was causing the ruckus. It was a giant or rather a giantess. There was nowhere for them to hide. They could do nothing but wait for the being to arrive and hope it was friendly.

As the figure got closer, they saw that the creature was almost as tall as the tallest trees and had bright red hair which was full of vines and branches and leaves and what may have been a bird's nest. She wore a huge red plaid dress and her feet were bare and coated with mud. Her skin was covered with scabs and thick dark hair.

Chapter 12

The Perfect Wish

Luke slung the pack off his shoulder and grabbed the book from it. But in his hurry to pull it open, he dropped it. Although Lucy was shaking, she lit and passed Luke the lamp and picked the book up, speedily thumbing through it to the last page they had read. The following page held an image of the being that was coming their way. The giantess stopped twenty feet in front of them and scratched her bird's nest of hair. Lucy turned the page and read, "If you meet the giantess Hochma, ask her what the perfect wish is." Lucy pointed to the words, and Luke looked at her and then at the giantess. He stuttered, "Wh..WWW What is the per perfect wish?"

Hochma growled, "Of course the perfect wish is for unlimited wishes."

Feeling that she was safe, Lucy spoke up to the giantess now and said with great joy, "Thank you Giantess Hochma, we will remember you when we receive our wishes."

Hochma replied in a sad tone, "I hope not," and with a downcast face walked away from them.

Chapter 13

War Breaks Out

Although confused by the creature's answer and reaction, Lucy and Luke were jumping up and down with happiness. They stopped and looked around to get their bearings and they picked up the lamp, recognizing that they were just a hop and skip away from the spring. They charged down the path and into the woods to the spot near the old fallen tree. They were gasping for air when they reached the spring, so they stopped to catch their breath, before making the first wish.

Lucy set the book down and Luke placed the lamp on the ground beside them. He said, "Lucy, be careful not to knock it over. Remember, when the lamp goes out we lose the gift." Luke announced, "OK spring, we're here for our wish". The water level dropped until it disappeared and they saw only gravel at the bottom of the spring. Lucy looked down into it worriedly. She said, "I hope something hasn't gone wrong. The rhyme says the spring will dry. Is that what is happening?"

In spite of this fear, she let out a huge sigh and picked up the book searching through the pages for the formula to make a wish. She came upon a picture of the spring and the words "Make the first wish, and make it right, make it wrong and there will be a fight." "I wonder what that means?" Lucy said.

Luke said, "I hope that we can handle it if we make the wrong wish."

"All we can do is try our best". Lucy replied. "Let's do it on the count of three." In unison they said," One, two, three. We wish for unlimited wishes!"

At once, thunder rolled, and the sound of screaming and loud noises broke out all around them. The trees shuddered and bent. Forest animals stampeded past them wild-eyed and terrified. The sky became dark and the children heard the sound and smell of gunfire close by. Once again Luke recalled his nightmare.

Chapter14

The Imbalance

Terrified, Lucy shouted into the air, "Stop!" but all the commotion continued. She tried again, "As above, so below. Stop! " The chaos and hubbub around them continued. The children saw something approaching them from out of the bushes. It was an old man. With the help of a carved wooden staff, he slowly made his way through the long willow branches towards them. He had a sack on his back. Over his shirt there was a raggedy old vest with many pockets on it. He stopped in front of them and with a long pained sigh said, "Are you happy now?"

The children looked at him and then at each other. They shook their heads. Lucy asked, "What do you mean? Who are you? What's going on?" They had to shout to be heard above the gunfire and screaming of woodland creatures.

The old man introduced himself as Chesed the herb peddler, and went on to recount the legend of the spring. He explained, "Every hundred years or so someone discovers the spring and tries to make the same wish. And every time this wish is made, war breaks out."

Luke said, "Why does war break out?"

Chesed replied, "Because whatever you wish for, everyone gets."

Luke asked, "Why does everyone get our wish and what does that have to do with a war?"

Chesed took a deep breath and answered, "Because the gift of the Tablet of Hermes includes the spell, 'As above, So below'."

Lucy shook her head in confusion and said, "So whatever we wish for, everyone gets?"

Luke scratched his head and asked, "But why won't the power of the Tablet stop This?"Luke waved his hands to point out the chaos all around them.

Chesed answered, "Because the power of the spring is stronger than the power of the Tablet."

Lucy said, "But why does war break out? I don't understand that."

Chesed answered, "Because if you get unlimited wishes, so does everyone else. And everyone wants stuff. Well it takes "stuff" to make more "stuff." One of the things used to create many things is trees. Trees are needed to build the houses, furniture and books that folks are wishing for. Another thing that will be needed to satisfy these wishes is land and lumber to build factories. That means that lots of trees will be cut and that all the plants and animals that live here and in other fields and forests will be left homeless or dead. It also means that creatures that ate these plants and took shelter here will have no food or place to feel safe and protected like you feel when you snuggle into your warm bed at night with a full belly.

"But why war?" Luke implored.

Chesed looked into Luke's eyes and answered, "Because everyone is fighting over who is going to get the land and the trees to have their wishes filled."

"But I thought it was magic. I thought the things we wished for just appeared," said Luke.

Chesed shaking his head sadly replied, "So does everyone else. But something never comes from nothing. There always needs to be a thing that the somethings are made from. That is the balance of nature."

Luke and Lucy both released a deep sigh. Lucy asked Chesed, "So what do we do now?"

Chesed said, "Go to the spring and take back the first wish and look for Tipareth, the old tamarack. She will help you do the right thing. She is the wisest tree in the forest." Luke groaned in dismay.

Chapter 15

Canceling the First Wish

What occurred to Lucy then was that they had not asked where Tipareth could be found. She looked up and saw that they were once more alone in the woods and worse yet, it seemed to be getting dark. It was even scarier that the thundering sound she thought was probably cannon, was getting closer. She didn't know for sure because, she had never heard cannon fire. But they both knew what gunfire sounded like because they sometimes heard hunters in the woods near their home. But the most frightening fact was noticing the oil was nearly gone from the glass bottom of the lamp.

Shouting over the bedlam around them Luke implored, "I wonder if this will use up our second wish?"

Waving her arms and wincing at the chaos of noise and the smell of gunpowder, Lucy replied, "It doesn't matter Luke. We started this and we are the only ones who can stop it." On the count of three again."

Together they repeated, "One, two, three, we take back our wish, as above, so, below." The roar and smoke of guns was gone. The cries and howling of animals stopped. The forest returned to the way they had found it. They looked at each other fearfully. Luke said, "We are going to have to be very careful. I had no idea how one wish could cause so much trouble."

Lucy nodded and sighed in relief that the crisis around them had settled. She had never been as afraid in her life. Luke thought about telling Lucy his dream but was afraid that telling it would scare her even more.

Chapter 16

Tired and Hungry

Lucy said, "Now where are we supposed to find Tipareth?"

Luke answered, "I've had enough excitement for today. Let's go home."

Lucy replied, "I'm tired and hungry too Luke, but what about the gift of the tablet? Once the lamp goes out so does our power."

Luke gave her a look of disgust and answered, "I know you're right but I don't have to like it."

They sat down beside the tablet and pondered their problem in the fading light of the sun. Suddenly Lucy brightened up and said, "Why don't we see if the gift of the tablet can give us something to eat?"

Luke jumped up and said, "Right! Of course. We'll take some supper now Mr. Tablet." They waited. Nothing happened. They looked at each other in despair.

"OK," Lucy said. "I guess that isn't going to work."

Just then, Luke rubbed his tummy and said, "I'd do anything for an apple jelly sandwich right now." Low and behold into his hand appeared an apple jelly sandwich.

Lucy yelled "Yahoo! We need to say exactly what we want." Lucy said, "May I have a blueberry jam sandwich tablet?" Sure enough, into her hand appeared a jam sandwich. They ate their sandwiches with delight and then asked for oatmeal raisin cookies for dessert.

Chapter 17

Harnessing The Power of the Tablet

"OK", Luke said, "Let's see what all we can do with this power."

Lucy responded, "Good idea Luke, and then we'll know how we can use it when we need to." Luke whispered, "Let it snow." Snowflakes filled the air around them.

Lucy shouted, "No snow." The snow disappeared. They looked at each other in amazement. Lucy gasped, "Wow we could have been using this all along!"

Luke said, "I wonder if it will refill the oil in the lamp?"

Lucy said, "Top up the oil in the lamp." Nothing happened. "Too bad," said Luke.

Lucy said, "Now the next step is to find this Tipareth the Tamarack."

Chapter 18

Luke Studies the Book

Exhausted after all the excitement plus having a full belly, Lucy grew sleepy. She suggested that they each take a little nap while the other one thought up a plan to find the tamarack. Covering for his fear of going back into that horrible dream, Luke answered, "I'm too restless to nap, I'll plan while you sleep." She answered, "OK then," as she pulled the moss back into its place over the tablet. It not only made a good table but also a great little bed with that thick cushiony green moss She curled up on her side , head on arm using her sweater as a blanket.

Luke saw that the book was lying on a large flat rock near the spring and tiptoed over to get it. The sun was just about set now and the birds were singing their winding down songs. He returned to the moss-covered tree and lowered himself down beside it and pulling the lamp closer he studied the book as Lucy softly snored close by. Carefully paging through the book he looked for clues to where this mysterious tree might be.

Chapter 19

Lucy Hears Tapping

Lucy shifted and squirmed her body to find a comfortable position on the tablet. She was about to give up when she heard something. It was a rapid, tap tap tap tap tap tap. She sat up and looked around for Luke. He was gone. She heard the sound again, tap, tap, tap, pause tap, tap, tap. Then she recognized what was making the noise. It was a woodpecker. The sun was up now and she wondered where and why her brother had gone. She arose and gathered her sweater up and looked around for anything else that her brother may have left behind. The lamp was still sitting on the ground beside the tablet. The flame was out. Its oil was gone. She cried out desperately, "Luke, where are you?!" There was no reply except for more tapping. She searched the area around her. No sign of Luke. She walked toward the pathway along the stream.

She was starting to panic now, wondering if something bad had happened to her brother while she slept. When she finally reached the fallen log just in off the path, she heard the tap, tap, tap again. She searched around looking for that noisy bird. Then she realized that the tapping sound had changed. Now it had a deeper pitch. "What on earth are you eating mister woodpecker?" she thought out loud. There was a beating of wings and a crashing as the bird flew up through the tree tops and away. She walked over to the place from which he had risen. She saw where he had made a couple of fresh holes in the trunk of the fallen tree and then she noticed a shiny spot. On closer inspection, she saw (although she couldn't believe her eyes), a red stone. She touched it. It looked like what she thought was a ruby. She carefully checked out the tree trunk. There, was something that was made out of gold (at least that was what she thought it must be) and there were also green stones beside the red ones. Could these be emeralds wondered Lucy?

Just then, she felt something grab her by the shoulder and shake her. She screamed in fright as...

Chapter 20

Lucy's Dream

She opened her eyes and saw Luke looking down on her. She jumped up and scanned the forest realizing she had fallen asleep. She told Luke about the dream. He said, "Weird eh? A tree trunk with gold and jewels on it!" He began to explain to her what he had learned from the book. "While you were getting your beauty sleep" he teased, (as she swatted him on the arm), "I was learning how to use the tablet."

She replied, "Yes and what did you learn brainiac?" she chuckled.

"Well it's simple. I don't know why we didn't think of it earlier. We need to use our minds to make a picture of what we want and then the tablet will create it for us."

She slapped her forehead, and said "Of course. Great! OK tablet, how about giving us a map to Tamarack." And there appeared on the moss-covered tablet a map. The map showed where they were with the words, "U R Here," and Tamarack as X. There was the spring, the tablet, and to their amazement, only a few trees were between them and Tamarack.

They picked up the map and started off. The sun was set now so they were traveling in poor light. The moon was not yet up and the lamp only lit a small area around it because the wick was turned down so low to save the remaining oil. They walked southeast of the spring for three minutes before they recognized the pattern of trees on the map. They stopped. Lucy stood beside her brother and said, "Luke, you look from in front of you all the way around counter clockwise and I'll start looking at the trees in front of me all the way around, clockwise. That way, one of us should be able to spot the tree."

It was no easy task. Neither one of the children was sure what a tamarack tree looked like. They knew spruce by its sharp needles and fir by its soft needles and pine by its long needles. They knew many of the leafy trees like maple and poplar and willow and oak and the white barked birch, but tamarack wasn't a common tree in their neighbourhood. They continued scanning the tree bark and branches looking for something that would remind them of what a tamarack looked like. Finally Luke shouted, "I found it!"

Chapter 21

Tipareth

With the loudness of his voice, a bird flew off its night roost in terror. Lucy jumped both at Luke's volume and the crashing of wings through the branches. She joined him beside the tree. When she checked out the needles, she remembered that this tree had the softest ones and they turned yellow and dropped off before winter.

They regarded the lamp to see how much oil was there. There was very little. They knew by the rate it had been burning, that it would soon be gone. They looked at each other and at the tree. Lucy spoke first. "Are you Tipareth?" Nothing happened.

Then Luke pulled the book from his sack and turned pages madly. He stopped and said, "As above, so below. Wise Tipareth may we beg your council?"

The wind picked up again and they saw through the bare branches of the trees that a full moon had risen. A soft voice said, "It is I the Crone Tipareth. What is the council you need my dear ones?"

Luke and Lucy looked at each other in astonishment and then the lamp flickered out. "Oh no!" Lucy moaned. Panicking, Luke quickly tried to shake the lamp back to life without success.

Chapter 22

The REAL Perfect Wish

The soft voice repeated, "What is the council you need my dear ones?" Lucy almost cried with relief. Luke answered while Lucy held her breath, hoping they would be able to finish the quest without the oil.

 Luke said, "What is the perfect wish? And where is the Krown of Keter?"

The tree sighed and rocked as the wind blew through it. The children waited. Luke was afraid they would be limited to only one question.

Tipareth answered in two parts. She said, "The perfect wish is that everyone has what they need. But what does the Krown of Keter have to do with all of this?"

Lucy explained about the wishing spring granting two wishes and what happened when they made the first wish.

Chapter 23

The Royal Family

Luke asked again where the Krown of Keter could be found. Tipareth responded, "The Krown was brought home many years ago. The quest you have undertaken has already been fulfilled. The wishing spring was once in the garden of a giant castle. The royal family lived a very lavish life. They ate the best and wore the finest clothes and decorated their rooms with the grandest furniture. To be able to do this they had to cut down the trees to make beams and floors for the castle. They had to cut down the trees to grow the crops so they could eat their fill. They had to kill even more trees to build the furniture that graced the castle in such style. Soon all the trees were gone and all of the creatures who lived in that forest were gone because they lost their homes. The berries and nuts they lived on disappeared with the trees. When the trees are cut, the rain couldn't find a place to get into the earth and the land became a parched desert."

"Why?" asked Lucy.

Tipareth answered, "When the trees are cut down, the rain washes away with the precious topsoil because there are no leaves or roots to hold it in place. Then much of the rich topsoil that feeds the trees, animals and food that humans eat, runs away with the rain, and when the wind comes, even more of the top soil blows away because there are no roots, or bushes or moss to hold the precious dirt in place. Then seeds have no place to lay protected until they sprout and grow. " Surrounded by the forest, Luke and Lucy listened entranced trying to imagine a desert.

Chapter 24

Empty Bellies and A Daughter's Wish

Tipareth continued, "Soon there was no fresh water or food for the kingdom. They had fancy clothes to wear, gorgeous furniture to sit and sleep on, but nothing to eat in the great hall of the castle. The family brought all of their jewels to the table and looked upon them. But these jewels were hard and cold and the family was starving and thirsty.

Finally, in despair, the king's daughter went outside and cried when she could see nothing but desert all around them. The wonderful trees she'd played in and under only a few years earlier were gone. She spotted a royal blue feather on the ground and picked it up. Her mouth was dry as dust as she looked into the once beautiful now dried up spring in the old garden of the castle. She said to herself, "If this were a magic feather, I would wish for the forest to be back to the way it was before we were here." Suddenly the castle had vanished and the royal family found themselves surrounded by trees. They were so happy that they danced around and joyfully sang of songs praise to the trees.

The king found a tall straight pine tree and took off his krown and asked his son to climb up to the top of the tree and place the it there. The krown was made of gold and had eight rubies and eight emeralds in it. The son was surprised because the krown had been one of the treasures his father had been most fond of. But the prince climbed up the tree and placed the krown on the top.

That was almost one thousand years ago now. The queen said to her family, "That's where the Krown belongs because the real royalty here is the forest. We would have had nothing if the forest had not been here and yet we didn't respect our blessing until it was gone." The family that was once royal and full and then hungry and thirsty, remembered that the gold, rubies and emeralds were useless when they were starving. They were very lucky to have understood in time that the forest is the royalty of the world, for without trees we'd have no water, food or shelter."

Chapter 25

The Second Wish

"Thank you Tipareth but now we must make the second wish and get home. Our abba and ama will be very worried", said Lucy. The children started back. Even though it was dark, they were able to follow their earlier path and when they were confused they found an open spot in the trees and checked the map by the bright light of the full moon. Before long they were back at the spring.

It was full of water again now. Together they made the second wish on the count of three the children spoke the words, "As above so below. We wish that everyone has whatever they need." Then Luke reached for the leather pouch in his pocket and pulled out an offering of cornmeal and sprinkled it at the base of the spring. He recited the prayer of thanks taught to him by his grand ama and then placed the book and the lamp on a flagstone beside the spring. They turned and started down the now familiar path home.

Chapter 26

The Krown of Keter

When they came to the giant nurse tree, Lucy remembered her dream and began searching the trunk to see if this was the tree of her dream. Sure enough, about four feet from what would have been the top of the old tree, was the Krown of Keter, complete with its rubies and emeralds. The tree was so laden with moss and lichen that the krown wouldn't have been noticed if one didn't know what to look for.

The children were amazed at how long ago this tree had fallen and how it was still teaming with life. After all these years it nourished insects, woodpeckers, fungi, and housed squirrels and moles. As she pulled her prayer bag from her pocket and sprinkled an offering at the base of the tree, Lucy said, "Wow, I can hardly believe that this tree is over a thousand years old and still so rich with life.

Luke said, "I know. We are so blessed to have all of these trees and the creatures and plants that live among them. Now we are the royal subjects at the foot of the throne. And the throne is the forest."

As they climbed the tree once more and emerged on the path from the stream they saw that their abba and ama were waiting for them. They ran up to their parents talking over top of each other about all that had happened.

When the whole story had been told, their abba and ama each wrapped their free arm around a child and pulled them into a family hug smiling at each other over the children's shoulders. They were joyous that their young had learned the lesson that their Grand abbas and amas had taught them, one summer long ago.

The End

Grandmother Bina stood and carefully stretched her old aching bones. She said "Happy Birthday children.,

As they each wrapped an arm around her waist and snuggled into her side they answered, "Thank you for the very best gift in the world."

Jody-Jack added, "The Gift is knowing what a gift we have, when we all have what we need."

Jessie-Mae put in, "And, knowing that protecting this gift is worth far more than everyone having whatever they want.

Jody Jack plucked the apple from the window sill and passed it to his elder. She pronounced, "Thank you Mother Earth for our food", and after taking a small bite passed it to Jessie Mae. The girl repeated the thanks and took one bite and passed the fruit to her twin who did the same. The ritual of thanks was repeated with the cup of water from the window sill.

Finally Grandmother said, "As above , so below".

The Beginning.....###

ABOUT THE AUTHOR

I am a 54 year old wife, mother and grandmother who loves fiercely and advocates for the vulnerable and disenfranchised. I believe that humanity is on the verge of discovering that we are all connected and what we do to the earth and to each other, we do to ourselves. I have spent many years exploring the paradox of a Creator who draws us closer by stretching our faith through adversity in a game of Peek a Boo.

Thank you for reading my book. If you enjoyed it, won't you to leave me a review at your favourite retailer and check out my blog at http://sassimintgrace.wordpress.com.

Thanks

ABOUT THE ARTIST

I was born in Vermont, USA and have resided at St. Mary's first Nation in Fredericton for 37 years. I started painting in 2000, as I was turning60 years old and couldn't contain the desire any longer. I have created many, many paintings in acrylic on canvas. I have found the joy of being in a different place and finding pieces of myself within the work, sometimes unexpectedly.

Other Books By the Author

Published in 2012....

A Friend of a Friend

Prologue

48 hours from now

Six year old Peter woke up to a roaring noise and found himself in a dark tight space. His head ached, he was cold, hungry and needed to pee. He felt around in the dark. He didn't know if he should shout or not. Making a racket might get him hurt if he was still with the bad guys. The last thing he remembered was being put into the trunk of the bad man's car. There was a strong odor and he must have fell asleep. But this was a different place. The container he found himself in now, was much smaller and that awful smell was gone. He pushed gingerly out against the sides; it seemed to be cardboard but he couldn't find a place thin enough to break out of it. There were fine holes punched through here and there. He could feel cold air coming in through them. This was the vision that he'd woke up from the night before. It wasn't a nightmare; it was a prediction of the future, his future.

Coming soon....

Sassimint Versus

Memoir of a Poisoned Child

So here we go....

For the last ten or so years I have held the belief that I chose this life before I was born because it would afford me the opportunity to learn the spiritual lessons I needed or wanted , for my soul to 'ripen' so to speak.

I have led a charmed life. I have the luck of the shithouse rat. That means, nine out of ten times when I fall down the shithouse hole of life, I come out smelling like a rose. I can find patches of four leafed clover but my financial state has often left me vulnerable to loss of my basic security/survival needs. Yet in fact, I always have enough to share with many. This is a gift that I am grateful for and I hope to share some of my serendipitous happiness with you.

Many who know me are astonished to learn all that I have 'experienced' in my years. Some are amazed and others baffled by my Radical optimism about society and the future of the world.

This life certainly has given me ample lessons. In these pages I hope to be able to share my perspective with you and perhaps give you reason to take my notion of the prebirth selection of a life of my choosing into consideration.

Promise me one thing, don't stop until you reach the end. If you do, you'll miss the best parts.

Life in Fredericton New Brunswick Canada circa 1960

There were three main features in the living room or "Front room" as we referred to it as. The biggest object in there was a piano. My mum played that on Friday and Saturday nights when the family gathered around to drink beer, rum and play guitar and sing.

The next important piece was the TV set. I remember watching Ed Sullivan, Bewitched, Red Skelton and Carol Burnet. I can remember when JFK was shot and when men landed on the moon. I remember watching Shirley Temple, Francis The Talking Mule, and Abbot and Costello movies on Saturday mornings and The Bugs Bunny Show and The Beverly Hillbillies on Saturday evenings. The final significant piece of the Front room was dad's chair. It was the throne. It was a padded rocker that Grampy commanded from.

Some of my most vivid memories occurred in this room. At Christmas time the banisters and door cases were all decorated with fresh fir tips.

A homemade crow's foot wreath always graced out front door. The idea of an artificial tree never occurred to us. I remember the wonderful smell of evergreen and turkey cooking but the pleasantries of Christmas end here.

Without fail, Christmas was a time when my parents were drinking and fighting. There was either cold silence or violence between them on weekends and holidays. I cherished peaceful the Saturday morning TV while they slept off the previous night's rum and by supper time they had drank enough that they needed a nap before they could proceed with the night's buzz .This was when I got to enjoy Bugs Bunny and The Beverly Hillbillies.

One Christmas something really unsettling happened. There was a Jehovah's Witness minister that used to visit us sometimes. This Christmas morning he showed up with a little boy about my age and sat there with him and watched us open our presents. I didn't really understand why he was there but I wasn't comfortable with it. I knew that he didn't believe in Christmas because our grade two teacher was a JW and she wouldn't allow us a tree or a party. We felt bad about this but didn't get why she was being so mean. I felt that it was very cruel of Mr. Mullin to bring this child to our house to see us get gifts while I knew that he had none.

The last Christmas memory I had in this house was 1975. My uncle Bobby came in very late on Christmas eve under the influence of a lot of booze. My gram always cooked the turkey and peeled the vegetables on the eve before so that she wouldn't have to get up with a hangover and cook. My uncle decided that the turkey needed a little trimming up and spread spaghetti and meatballs all over it. Were Gram and Gramp ever mad when they got up in the morning and discovered this little prank. That was the last Christmas Bobby spent with our family. He died from alcoholism two years later.

The basement or "Cellar" was the next place that I have strong memories of. It was dark and dirt floored. There was a hole with water in it that held the sump pump and a cold storage area where pickles and root vegetables were shelved. This was an area that was filled with rich smells. There a rich scent of wet bamboo cane that was woven into the canoe seat frames that Grampy brought home from the factory where he worked. That was Chestnut Canoe Company, one of the most famous canoe manufacturing companies in the world at that time. He also had buckets of hide strips to string snowshoes and skowhegan to protect that hide.

Finally we arrive at the yard. In warm weather, I spent most of my waking hours outside. The front right corner of our yard held a driveway to the garage and behind that was a vegetable garden. On the other side of the property was a big spruce tree that was tall enough to see out the window of the upstairs window of my brothers' room.

Down the middle of the backyard was a path that lead to the chicken house. This small building generally housed several dozen chickens and usually held a pig or two, a couple of turken-geese as well as some white New Zealander rabbits.

I grew up collecting eggs, and watching some of them hatch. I remember the piglets coming home and the adults getting made into bacon. We also used the rabbits for meat. At an early age I participated in the process of slaughtering and cleaning livestock. The rest of the yard behind the lawn at the back of the house was woods. There was a homemade brick barbecue on the opposite corner from the garden. My grandfather and I spent many pleasant evenings there. He showed me how to make a mosquito smudge with dry sticks, bark and fresh grass.

The front yard was very boggy which supported a huge weeping willow tree. Even in the height of summer heat there was warm moist moss growing under that big tree.

Behind that are was a patch of woods that I spent a lot of time in. I found an old wood stove at had been thrown away and made it the central piece in my 'camp'. I had a bunch of tin cans and other junk that

I pretended was my house stuff and spent the lion's share of my days playing alone there.

And the newest novel..........still in utero.....

Hope's Kiss

Prologue

4021 suicides reported in the Tri State area. The majority of these were executed en mass at local churches although there were also 896 individual acts confirmed at this time. These were simultaneously carried out on October 31st.

Sources indicate that the groups and individuals involved were part of an online site promoting the belief that the world economy is on the verge of collapse and therefore all personal security and social infrastructure will soon deteriorate or dissolve. Rather than suffer the potential fascist chaos of what some proclaim is the imminent 'End of the World', those involved chose self imposed extinction via lethal injection.......

They took your computer and all of your papers. There were U.S. officials in and out of our place for the last three days. What could they be thinking? Terrorism? For God's sake, of all things. You wouldn't believe the paperwork I had to fill out to get in here today. They practically wanted me to sign over my car. Oh and by the way, they have frozen our bank accounts. Something about the Homelands Security Act .How in hell could we be charged under American laws?